This Book Belongs to:

If it doesn't challenge you, it won't

It Always
Seems
Impossible
Until
It's Done

JUST
BELIEVE
IN YOUR
DREAMS

Good
things
take
time

Don't you give up now. Keep pushing, keep believing, keep fighting

If
Life gives
you
lemons
make
Lemonade

CREATE
Something
TODAY
EVEN
IF·IT
Sucks

We went
through a
lot of stuff
to get to
where we

It doesn't mather if people like you or not. The right

You have tons of experience now so you are well equipped to move ahead.

BE THE
PERSON
YOU
WANT TO HAVE
IN YOUR
life

WHATEVER YOU DECIDE TO DO IN LIFE, MAKE SURE IT MAKES YOU happy

NEVER
MEASURE
YOUR
PROGRESS
USING
SOMEONE
ELSE'S RULER

THE
BEST
project
YOU WILL EVER
WORK ON
is your
self

OLD WAYS
WON'T
OPEN NEW
DOORS

ENERGY
SPEAKS
LOUDER
THAN
WORDS

TRAIN
YOUR MIND
TO SEE THE GOOD
IN EVERY
SITUATION

You are
who you
choose to

No one is you and that is your super power

I AM IN
THE PROCESS
OF BECOMING
THE BEST
VERSION OF
MYSELF

Stop
Talking
Start
Doing

believe
in yourself
you are
stronger
than you
think

you
ARE
stronger
THAN
YOU
think

some people
are going to
reject you
simply because
you shine too
bright
that's okay;
keep shining

a little step
may be
the beginning
of a great
journey

Everything
will
be Ok

BE THE
reason
SOMEONE
Smiles
TODAY

a
Winner
is a
Dreamer
who never
Gives up

WORK HARD
IN
Silence
LET YOUR
Success
BE
YOUR NOISE